LOWER YOUR CHOLESTEROL IN 30 DAYS

LOWER YOUR CHOLESTEROL IN 30 DAYS

ABRIDGED FROM *BIO-NUTRONICS*

by *Emanuel Cheraskin*, M.D., D.M.D.,
and *Neil S. Orenstein*, Ph.D.,
with *Paul L. Miner*

A PERIGEE BOOK

Perigee Books
are published by
The Putnam Publishing Group
200 Madison Avenue
New York, NY 10016

Lower Your Cholesterol in 30 Days is an abridgment of
Bio-Nutrionics: Lower Your Cholesterol in 30 Days,
published in 1986 by The Putnam Publishing Group.

Library of Congress Cataloging–in–Publication Data

Cheraskin, E. (Emanuel), date.
Lower your cholesterol in 30 days / by Emanuel Cheraskin
and Neil S. Orenstein, with Paul L. Miner.

p. cm.
"A Perigee book."
1. Low-cholesterol diet.   2. Low-cholesterol diet—Recipes.
I. Orenstein, Neil S.   II. Miner, Paul L.   III. Title.
RM237.75.C49   1989   89-3896 CIP
613.2′8—dc20
ISBN 0-399-51555-0

Text design by Beth Tondreau Design

Printed in the United States of America
1   2   3   4   5   6   7   8   9   10

Contents

Acknowledgments

We'd like to thank Stanley J. Liefer, Diane Borho/Maureen Byrne, Sandy Hirsch, Paula Shabman, Sondra Tarica, Dr. William Castelli, Giant Foods Corporation, The American Heart Association, The U.S. Department of Agriculture, The National Heart, Lung and Blood Institute, Dr. and Mrs. Donald Rudin, Ayers Art Studio of Baltimore, and our editor, Judy Linden.

A special thanks for selected recipes from The Culinary Arts Center, Lenox, Massachusetts, and Sarah L. Bingham, M.S., Director.

LOWER YOUR CHOLESTEROL IN 30 DAYS

Introduction

The Promise of This Book

By following the program outlined here you *can* lower your high blood cholesterol in thirty days without the aid of medication of any kind. You also will begin to reach your ideal weight for your height and build; regain energy, stamina, and vitality you may not have felt in years; and—most important—dramatically reduce your risk factors for cardiovascular disease. We guarantee you will feel terrific! With these improvements, you can't help but have a more positive attitude . . . be more confident and self-assured.

The program is already endorsed by thousands of people, including world champion tennis player Ivan Lendl. Called Bio-Nutrionics, it produces results in a short but realistic period of time. These results are so significant that they prompted us to write this book. We want you, too, to discover the difference Bio-Nutrionics can make.

Take This Book Seriously

If you do, it will fulfill its promise.

Our most recent study of 104 male and 64 female subjects on the Bio-Nutrionics Program with an age range between fifteen and seventy-five (a mean age of forty-two) shows an average reduction of cholesterol of 10 percent in the first thirty days of the program.

What does this mean to you? According to medical authorities, a 1 percent reduction in blood cholesterol results in a *2 percent reduction* in *coronary risk*. Therefore, the people on the plan reduced their risk of cardiovascular diseases (which include high blood pressure, stroke, and coronary disease) by 20 percent in thirty days!

We ask that you make a serious commitment to your own personal health and well-being. The life-style modifications outlined in this book are not drastic and they *will* work for you. But they do require your complete participation to be effective. The most important qualification you need to succeed is the determination to take control of your own health. And you're worth it!

1

Cholesterol Overload: The Enemy of Your Health

What Is Cholesterol?

Cholesterol is a white, sticky, fatlike, tasteless and odorless substance necessary to all of our cells. It is carried in our bloodstream, and found in all foods of animal origin.

From the day we're born we begin taking cholesterol into our body in the foods we eat. That is one source of cholesterol.

Our second source of cholesterol is the body itself, which produces a steady supply of it in our intestinal tract and in our liver. Day in and day out throughout our lifetime we continue this process of both ingesting and manufacturing cholesterol. When we eat high quantities of cholesterol the body responds by manufacturing less. When we eat too little cholesterol the body responds by producing more. Remarkable, isn't it?

Cholesterol is important to your overall health. It serves as raw material for the creation of cell membranes, bile acids, and sex hormones. Nine tenths of all the cholesterol in our bodies is located in the cells. A major part of our total cholesterol supply is used in the continuous process of regenerating and rebuilding body cells.

However, as important as cholesterol is to maintaining a healthy body, research reveals that far more people than ever suspected are at high risk of heart attack and stroke because of cholesterol overload.

The medical term for this affliction is "hypercholesterolemia." It means we have more cholesterol in our blood than is consistent with good health. This may be the result of eating too many high-cholesterol foods or the body producing too much or eliminating too little cholesterol.

Cholesterol overload is the first stage of a condition that progressively leads to atherosclerosis, commonly called hardening of the arteries. Atherosclerosis in turn contributes to coronary heart disease, or CHD.

For years many of us have been assured by our doctors that our cholesterol levels were "within normal range." With that assurance we paid little attention to our blood cholesterol level until it reached 250 or higher. At that point our doctor usually sounded the alarm and we searched frantically to find a way to undo the damage. But by 1984, it was accepted that excessive buildup of fats and cholesterol in our arteries is a primary cause of coronary artery disease. The time had finally arrived for the medical establishment to mount an all-out campaign against the nation's number-one killer.

The chart on page 13 shows existing cholesterol levels in adults and the recommended, or safe, cholesterol levels for the same group.

The broken line on the right shows that the mean cholesterol level for an adult American is currently at 210. A "safe" cholesterol level is in the 150–170 range. Dr. William

Castelli, director of the Framingham Study, has stated that he has never seen a case of CHD in an individual whose cholesterol level is at 150 or lower.

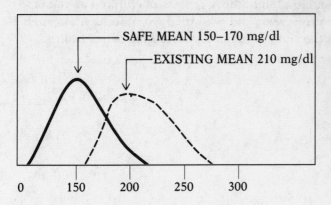

Are You a Candidate for CHD?

The answer is *Yes* if you fall into one or more of these categories.

1. If you're over thirty years of age and your cholesterol is over 170, you should take immediate steps to reduce your risk.

2. After the age of fifty the risk of CHD becomes greater for both men and women. So practically everyone over fifty should examine their diet and life-style and make the appropriate changes recommended in this book.

3. If your blood pressure is high (over 140/80), you should immediately reduce your risk factors.

4. Regardless of your gender, if you are ten pounds or more overweight you should apply the Bio-Nutrionics nutrition approach to risk-factor reduction.

5. Women approaching menopause should consider risk-factor reduction.

As you read over these categories, the important fact to remember is that coronary heart disease is exactly that—a disease. It can be prevented. Most important, *it is not a natural part of the aging process*. Evidence of the disease has been found in autopsy reports of children as young as two or three years old who died from accidental causes. Now is the time to prepare yourself for better health.

2

The Bio-Nutrionics Program to Cholesterol Reduction

Your Personal Risk Analysis Questionnaire

Begin the program with our personal risk factor questionnaire which begins on page 16. It asks you for your appraisal of your current diet and life-style. For the sake of your health, please be honest and forthright in your answers. No one except you will see them unless you wish to show the questionnaire to your doctor, a friend, or family member for discussion of the program. Your answers will help you judge if you're at risk now, and whether after thirty days on the program you have succeeded in reducing your CHD risk factors.

Begin our questionnaire by entering your answers to the twelve questions in the column headed "Start of Program." The questions deal with weight, blood pressure, physical activity, blood sugar, stress, and diet. Each question is numbered. You have a choice of answers listed under each question. Each is given a "point value" which is listed under the column labeled "Point Value." Read each answer carefully and then select the one that best describes your condition. Make sure you select only one answer to each question and be sure you enter the plus sign or minus sign in front of the point value when you enter it in the "Start of Program" column. When you are done, add up the total of plus and minus points and enter that total as "your total score" at the end of the questionnaire.

Personal Risk Factor Questionnaire

	Point Value	Start of Program	After 30 Days
1. Weight			
A. Underweight or normal	0	_____	_____
B. Overweight with no weight loss in last thirty days	+10	_____	_____
C. Overweight with loss of 3 pounds or more in last thirty days	+5	_____	_____
2. Blood Pressure			
A. Blood pressure normal (140/80 or lower) or you are taking blood-pressure medications	0	_____	_____

	Point Value	Start of Program	After 30 Days
B. Blood pressure high (over 140/80). Not taking medication and your blood pressure has not come down in the last thirty days	+10	_____	_____
C. Blood pressure high (over 140/80). Not taking medication, but your blood pressure has come down significantly in the last thirty days	+5	_____	_____
3. Exercise			
A. No *regular* exercise (less than five times per week)	+10	_____	_____
B. Mild exercise equal to walking half an hour a day at least five times a week	−5	_____	_____
C. Aerobic exercise at least twenty minutes four times per week	−15	_____	_____
4. Blood Sugar			
A. Have you ever been told that your blood sugar is too high (greater than 130 mg/dl)?	+10	_____	_____
B. Blood sugar is normal	0	_____	_____

	Point Value	Start of Program	After 30 Days
C. Do not know if blood sugar is normal	0	_____	_____
5. Smoking Habits			
A. Currently smoke a pipe or cigar	+5	_____	_____
B. Smoke less than one pack of cigarettes a day	+5	_____	_____
C. Smoke more than one pack of cigarettes a day	+10	_____	_____
D. Do not smoke now but have smoked in the last year	0	_____	_____
E. Never smoked, or used to smoke but have not smoked in the last year	−5	_____	_____
6. Stress			
A. I am "high-strung" and react strongly to stressful situations (type A behavior)	+5	_____	_____
B. Sometimes I'm "high-strung" and sometimes I'm calm	0	_____	_____
C. I am basically a calm person and do not react to stressful situations in an extreme manner	−5	_____	_____

	Point Value	Start of Program	After 30 Days
7. Dietary Fat Consumption (red meats, fried and fatty foods, eggs and dairy products)			
A. Above average	+10	_____	_____
B. Average	+5	_____	_____
C. Below average	−10	_____	_____
8. Vegetable Consumption			
A. Above average	−5	_____	_____
B. Average	+5	_____	_____
C. Below average	+10	_____	_____
9. Consumption of Unprocessed Cereal Grains (brown rice and whole-wheat products)			
A. Above average	−5	_____	_____
B. Average	+5	_____	_____
C. Below average	+10	_____	_____
10. Consumption of Refined Sugar in Foods such as Soft Drinks, Candies and Pastries			
A. Above average	+10	_____	_____
B. Average	+5	_____	_____
C. Below average	0	_____	_____
11. Consumption of fried foods and packaged foods containing "hydrogenated oil" such as potato chips, breaded and fried chicken or fish, and margarine is:			

	Point Value	Start of Program	After 30 Days
A. Above average	+10	_____	_____
B. Average	+5	_____	_____
C. Below average	−5	_____	_____

12. Are you currently engaged in a program to change your lifestyle (including nutritional and exercise components) in order to reduce your risk of CHD?

	Point Value	Start of Program	After 30 Days
A. Yes	−10	_____	_____
B. No	0	_____	_____
YOUR TOTAL SCORE		_____	_____

Now check the chart below to discover your current state of health.

If your number is	Your risk level is
−31 to −60	extremely low
0 to −30	low
+1 to +30	moderate
+31 to +60	high
+61 and above	extremely high

At the end of the first month, retake the questionnaire, filling out the column headed "After 30 Days." At that time add up and compare your total with the one you had before starting the program. The numbers will tell you immediately how well you're progressing. And if you are following our plan seriously, we guarantee you will move into a risk category at least one level lower than when you first began Bio-Nutrionics.

Smoking

If you stop smoking *now* you begin reducing risk factors immediately. We mention smoking here because it is the only habit discussed in your questionnaire that cannot be modified by altering diet or exercise. It is a life-style change you must be responsible for. Stopping smoking will reduce your risk of CHD to a greater degree than any other single change!

We hope that you stop smoking because if you do your efforts will be doubly rewarding.

3

The Nutrition Plan

Foods to Eat and Foods to Avoid

In the diagrams on page 24, you will see a comparison of
the typical American diet and the Bio-Nutrionics Plan.
They show you visually the difference between how you
now eat and a more healthful way of eating.

Listed below is a summary of the dietary changes you
should make to reduce your risk of CHD.

1. Sharply reduce your intake of foods high in saturated fats.
2. Double your consumption of complex carbohydrates, including foods high in fiber.
3. Satisfy your craving for sweets with fruits and
   other naturally sweet foods.
4. Limit red meat to three times a week in portions

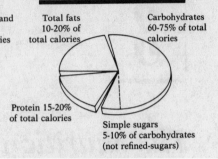

Typical American Diet

Total fats 40% of total calories

Carbohydrates and refined sugars 40-50% of calories

Protein 20-30% of total calories

Bio-Nutrionics Nutrition Plan

Total fats 10-20% of total calories

Carbohydrates 60-75% of total calories

Protein 15-20% of total calories

Simple sugars 5-10% of carbohydrates (not refined-sugars)

1. Excessively high in total fats.
2. Very low in complex carbohydrates.
3. High in refined sugars.
4. Very high in protein.

1. Sharply reduced fat consumption.
2. Increased intake of complex carbohydrates, grains, legumes and whole foods.
3. Sharply reduced consumption of refined sugars.
4. Moderately reduced consumption of protein.

up to 4 ounces after cooking, and limit eggs to a total of six per week.

5. Reduce the amount of dairy products that you normally eat.

The Fats in Our Diet

To reduce high blood cholesterol the Nutrition Plan calls for an immediate sharp reduction in dietary fats.

Let's learn the difference between the undesirable fats and the desirable fats.

Saturated Fats, the Undesirable Fat: These are the fats that come from animal sources. Saturated fats are typically solid at room temperature. Lard, butter, and animal meat contain lots of saturated fat and contribute to cholesterol overload.

Unsaturated Fats, the Desirable Fat: These fats are usually liquid at room temperature. There are two classifications of unsaturated fats that are distinguishable from each other by their chemical makeup. For our purposes we need to know that one type is monounsaturated fat, like olive oil, while the other is polyunsaturated fat, often identified as PUFA. Both are beneficial and allowable in the eating plan.

Dangerous Man-made Fats: A dangerous, man-made group of fats is created when unsaturated fats are hydrogenated by adding the chemical hydrogen to an oil. The molecular structure of the oil is changed in a way that keeps it from becoming rancid and gives it longer shelf life.

If the words "hydrogenated" or "partially hydrogenated" appear on the label, avoid using the product.

Which Fat Is Best for Cooking?

The best all-around oil for cooking is olive oil. It is stable at higher temperatures and does not "oxidize," or become rancid, easily. The polyunsaturated oils are not to be used for cooking. They oxidize when heated and should be used "cold" as in salad dressings.

Regardless of which oil you use, please remember that deep frying of any kind should be avoided.

Avoid Foods That Are Processed and Contain Refined Sugar

The Bio-Nutrionics Program emphasizes foods that are natural, whole, and unprocessed.

Foods that are processed or refined have been literally taken apart and then put back together. All the valuable nutrients are not put back in. For example, in the process of making white flour, the fiber and bran portion of wheat is separated and discarded from the kernel. The resulting white "flour" is a plain starch that has very little nutritional value other than calories.

When we talk about sweets, we should be aware that there are refined sugars and unrefined sugars. The refined sugars are simple sugars which have been stripped of all other nutrients, unlike the unrefined sugars in fruits, which nature packages along with fiber, vitamins, and minerals. So we ask you to avoid refined sugars such as those found in candy and soda pop. The energy burst you get from refined sugar (like chocolate) is only temporary. If you have a craving for sweets, eat a piece of fruit or try one of the desserts in our recipe section for an after-dinner treat.

Fiber in Our Diet:
What It Is, What It Does, and Why We Need It

What is fiber? It is the undigestible portion of food which is not absorbed by our bodies. It is a substance that promotes regularity, stabilizes blood-sugar levels, and lessens the risk of heart disease and colon cancer. Bran, apples, all grains—including brown rice—and green vegetables all contain significant amounts of fiber. Yet be alert that some fibers outperform others. One is oat bran, a delicious hot cereal that nutritionists believe can reduce cholesterol levels with surprising speed. One cup of oat bran as a daily breakfast cereal can reduce low-density lipoproteins in a single month by 10 percent in some individuals. Anyone with high cholesterol should consider this approach along with the rest of the program to lower cholesterol and increase stamina.

Plan Your Daily Meals From Six Food Groups

You'll be eating a recommended number of daily servings from each of six food groups that are listed.

By doing this you will enjoy healthy, balanced, nutritious meals every day.

Food Group 1: The Mineral Vegetables

Dark green leafy vegetables like spinach, kale, lettuce, and broccoli are high in minerals, such as magnesium and potassium (which effect blood-pressure regulation) and calcium (which helps prevent osteoporosis). Magnesium is contained in the green coloring matter of plants called chlorophyll. Chlorophyll is similar to the hemoglobin in our blood. As a matter of fact, chlorophyll and hemoglobin are almost identical except that chlorophyll contains magnesium and hemoglobin contains iron.

We know from both scientific study and general knowledge that people living on vegetarian diets have far lower risk factors for CHD. We are not necessarily suggesting that you become a vegetarian, but we are emphasizing the health-promoting benefits of vegetables high in minerals.

Food Group 2: Grains and Carbohydrate Vegetables

Carbohydrate food will make up as much as 60 to 75 percent of your Nutrition Plan. The largest portion of your carbohydrate intake will be from food list 2 on page 34. This list contains food from plant sources that are high in fiber and high in starch, known as complex carbohydrates. Whole grains are included in this food group. They are one of nature's finest sources of complex carbohydrates.

Food Group 3: Fruits

These are unrefined simple carbohydrates and will make up between 5 percent and 10 percent of your total carbohydrate food consumption. By eating the recommended daily servings of fruit you will be able to sharply reduce your intake of refined sugar. Fruits rank high on our list of whole foods. They will maintain your energy level and satisfy your hunger between meals.

Food Group 4: Dairy Foods

We urge you to stay well within the guidelines in this food group. It is very easy to increase your saturated fat intake with dairy foods, so be careful. Be sure to purchase cheese made from part-skim milk or low-fat milk. The hard cheeses like Parmesan are the best because they provide a lot of flavor in a small serving. The best food in this group is active yogurt because it replenishes the beneficial bacteria, lactobacillus, in your intestines. Be sure to buy plain active-culture low-fat yogurt.

Food Group 5: Protein

You will be eating far less protein than is found in the typical American diet. Most of us eat high-protein diets in the mistaken notion that protein is a high-energy food.

Protein is important for growth, maintaining body tissue, regulating water balance, and forming essential body compounds. But excess protein does increase the risk of osteoporosis.

Food Group 6: Desserts, Snacks, Condiments, and Beverages

This food list is filled with delicious, nutritious treats like nuts, which are a rich source of nutrients. But make sure you buy unsalted nuts and stop eating them before you exceed the recommended limits. This section also puts alcoholic beverages in perspective. Our commonsense position is that alcohol is generally more harmful to the body than it is beneficial. Our strongest recommendation is that you limit your intake of liquor, wine, or beer to two servings a day at the very most.

Calories Count:
But You Don't Have to Count Them

You may wish to know the number of calories in a servin
in each food group so they are listed below:

Food Group	Calories per serving
1. Mineral Vegetables	50
2. Grains and Carbohydrate Vegetables	100
3. Fruits	50
4. Dairy	100
5. Protein	50
6. Desserts, Snacks, Beverages	100

We have used these calorie values per serving to make
sure you are eating the correct number of portioned servings from each food list according to the weight recommended for your height and body build. *You simply count
servings, NOT CALORIES.*

How to Find Your Recommended Weight and Plan Your Daily Menus

On pages 30 and 31 you will find charts of recommended
weights for men and women. Decide whether you are a
person of small frame, medium frame, or large frame. Run
your finger down the chart until you find your height, then
move across until you come to the correct frame size. (A
man 5'10" tall of medium frame will have a recommended
weight of 155, and a woman 5'6" tall of small frame has a
recommended weight of 125 pounds.)

Now that you have found your recommended weight,
move right along to the charts on the following pages.
There's one for men and one for women. Please make sure
you use the correct chart.

Run your finger down the recommended-weight column

MEN

Recommended Weight for Your Height and Build*

Height Feet	Inches	Small Frame	Medium Frame	Large Frame
5	2	130	135	145
5	3	135	135	145
5	4	135	140	150
5	5	135	140	150
5	6	140	145	155
5	7	140	150	155
5	8	145	150	160
5	9	145	155	165
5	10	150	155	165
5	11	150	160	170
6	0	155	165	175
6	1	155	165	180
6	2	160	170	185
6	3	165	175	190
6	4	170	180	195

*The men's chart includes 5 pounds of clothing to be worn when stepping on the scale.

on the left and you will find in the columns to the right of your weight the number of recommended daily servings you should eat in each of the six food groups.

Food Group 1: Mineral Vegetables

Each 1-cup serving provides 50 calories unless noted otherwise in the list below.

Artichoke
Asparagus
Bamboo shoots

Beet greens
Beets
Broccoli

WOMEN

Recommended Weight for Your Height and Build*

Height				
Feet	Inches	Small Frame	Medium Frame	Large Frame
4	10	105	115	125
4	11	110	120	125
5	0	110	120	130
5	1	115	125	130
5	2	115	125	130
5	3	120	130	140
5	4	120	130	140
5	5	125	135	145
5	6	125	135	150
5	7	130	140	150
5	8	130	140	155
5	9	135	145	160
5	10	140	145	160
5	11	140	145	165
6	0	145	155	165

*The women's chart includes 3 pounds of clothing and 1" in height for low heels worn when stepping on the scale.

Brussels sprouts
Cabbage
Carrot greens
Carrots
Cauliflower
Celery
Chard
Collard greens
Cucumber
Dandelion greens
Eggplant

Green sweet peppers
Kale
Kelp
Kohlrabi
Mushrooms
Mustard greens
Okra
Onions
Parsley
Peppers
Radishes

MEN

Recommended Number of Portions to Eat Per Day in Each Food Group

The portions have been determined by your recommended weight shown in the left-hand column.

Recom-mended Weight	1 Mineral Vegeta-bles	2 Grains and Carbohy-drate Vegetables	3 Fruit	4 Dairy	5 Protein	6 Desserts, Snacks, Beverages
120	6	5	2	1	5	2
125	6	5	2	1	6	2
130	6	5	2–3	1	6	2
135	6	5–6	3	1	6	2
140	6	6	3	1	6	2
145	6	6	3	1–2	6	2
150	6	6	3	2	6	2
155	6	6	3	2	6	2–3
160	6	6	3	2	6	3
165	6	6	3	2	7	3
170	7	6	3	2	7	3
175	7	6–7	3	2	7	3
180	7	7	3	2	7	3
185	7	7	3	2	7	3–4
190	7	7	3	2	7	4
195	7	7	3	2	8	4
200	8	7	3	2	8	4
205	8	7–8	3	2	8	4
210	8	8	3	2	8	4
215	8	8	4	2	8	4
220	8	8	4	2	8	4–5
225	8	8	4	2	8	5
230	8	8	5	2	8	5
235	8	8–9	5	2	8	5
240	8	9	5	2	8	5
245	8	9–10	5	2	8	5
250	8	10	5	2	8	5

WOMEN

Recommended Number of Portions to Eat Per Day in Each Food Group

The portions have been determined by your recommended weight shown in the left-hand column.

Recom-mended Weight	*1* Mineral Vegeta-bles	*2* Grains and Carbohy-drate Vegetables	*3* Fruit	*4* Dairy	*5* Protein	*6* Desserts, Snacks, Beverages
90	4–5	3	2	1	4	1
95	5	3	2	1	4	1
100	5	3–4	2	1	4	1
105	5	4	2	1	4	1
110	5	4	2	1	4	1–2
115	5	4	2	1	4	2
120	5	4	2	1	5	2
125	6	4	2	1	5	2
130	6	4–5	2	1	5	2
135	6	5	2	1	5	2
140	6	5	2	1	5–6	2
145	6	5	2–3	1	6	2
150	6	5	3	1	6	2
155	6	5–6	3	1	6	2
160	6	6	3	1	6	2
165	6	6	3	1–2	6	2
170	6	6	3	2	6	2
175	6	6	3	2	6	2–3
180	6	6	3	2	6	3

Red cabbage
Rhubarb
Romaine lettuce (and other
  dark-green leafy lettuce)
Scallions
Soups (noncreamed, vege-
  table only)
Spinach
Sprouts
String beans

Summer squash
Swiss chard
Tomato sauce (⅓ cup)
Tomatoes
Turnip greens
All vegetable juices
Water chestnuts
Watercress
Zucchini

> **NOTE:** One serving of salad should equal 2 cups (2 portions). So by having a salad for both lunch and dinner you are eating 4 daily portions of mineral vegetables. You are also eating whole foods that are uncooked, so they have retained the greatest part of their vitamin and mineral content. We suggest that you shop the farmer's markets where growers are selling direct to consumers. You'll discover fresher foods, fresher vegetables in season, and a variety of better quality items at lower prices than those offered in grocery stores and supermarkets.

Food Group 2: Grains and Carbohydrate Vegetables

Each 1-cup serving provides 100 calories unless noted otherwise in the list below.

Barley, ½ cup
Beans, ½ cup
Blackeyed peas, ½ cup
Bran muffin, ⅓ muffin
  (1 ounce)
Brown rice, ½ cup

Buckwheat, ½ cup
Bulgur, ½ cup
Cassava
Cold cereal, 1 ounce
Cornbread, 2 × 2-inch square
Corn flour, ¼ cup

Cornmeal, ½ cup
Corn muffin, ⅓ muffin
  (1 ounce)
Corn on cob, 1 small
Crackers, 4
Dried peas or beans, ½ cup
English muffin, ½
Frijoles (beans), 3 ounces
Garbanzo beans (chick-
  peas), ½ cup
Granola (made without
  butter or oil), ½ cup
Green peas (fresh), 1 cup
Grits, ⅔ cup
Hot cereal
Jicama
Kasha (made with little or
  no oil)
Kidney beans, ½ cup
Lentils, ½ cup
Lima beans, ½ cup
Millet, ½ cup
Mung beans, ½ cup
Nacho chips, 10 chips
Navy beans, ½ cup
Oatmeal, ¾ cup
Parsnips
Pasta, ½ cup (whole-grain,
  artichoke, spinach)
Pinto beans, ½ cup
Plantain
Popcorn (air-popped),
  1 quart
Potato flour, ⅓ cup

Pumpkin
Red beans, ½ cup
Rice cakes, 3
Rice flour, ¼ cup
Rutabaga
Rye berries
Rye flour, ¼ cup
Sorghum, 1 cup
Soups, ¾ cup (meatless,
  noncreamed bean, and
  legumes)
Soybeans, ½ cup
Soybean flour, ½ cup
Spaghetti squash
Succotash, ½ cup
Sweet potato, ⅓ cup
Taco shells, 2 small
Tortilla, 1 6-inch round
Tortilla flour, 1 ounce
Triticale
Wheat berries
White potato, 1 medium
  (with skin)
Whole-grain bread, 1 slice
Whole-wheat bagel, ½
Whole-wheat bread, 1 slice
Whole-wheat pita bread,
  1 pocket (1½ ounce)
Whole-wheat roll, 1 small
Wild rice, ¾ cup
Winter squash
Yams, ½ cup
Yellow rose potato, 1 small

NOTE: Don't believe what you may have heard about pasta being fattening. It's the heavy, oily sauces many people use on pasta that have given it that reputation.

Remember that a large dish of pasta (2 cups) uses 2 of your daily grain and carbohydrate portions. It is commonly thought that potatoes, a starch like pasta, also are fattening—but that's not true either. Add variety to your diet with grits, kasha, an assortment of beans, and the flavor of vegetables like parsnips and rutabaga.

Food Group 3: Fruits

Each serving provides about 50 calories and the serving size is noted next to each fruit listed below.

Apple, 1 small
Apple juice, ½ cup
Applesauce (unsweetened), ½ cup
Banana, ½
Black currants (raw), ¾ cup
Blackberries, ½ cup
Blueberries, ½ cup
Cantaloupe, ⅓ small melon
Carambola, 1 small
Casaba melon, 2-inch wedge
Cherimoya, 2 ounces
Cherries, 10
Coconut (fresh), ½ ounce

Cranberries (raw), 1 cup
Cranberry sauce, ¼ cup
Dates, 2
Dried apricots, 5 halves
Dried figs, 1
Dried fruit, 2 pieces
Fresh apricots, 3
Fresh figs, 2
Fresh orange juice, ½ cup
Fruit cocktail (water-packed), ⅔ cup
Grapefruit, ½ medium
Grapes, 12
Guava, 1 medium
Honeydew, 1 2-inch wedge
Juice (unsweetened), ½ cup

Kiwi, 1 medium
Kumquats (raw), 4
Lavender gem, 1 medium
Lemon, unlimited
Loquat (raw), 10 medium
Lychees (raw), 10 medium
Mango (raw), ½ medium
Nectarine, 1 medium
Orange, 1 medium
Papaya, ½ medium
Peach, 1 medium

Persimmon, ½ medium
Pineapple(fresh, diced), ⅔ cup
Plums, 2 medium
Prunes, 2
Raisins, 2 tablespoons
Raspberries, ½ cup
Rosehips (fresh), ½ cup
Strawberries, 1 cup
Tangerine, 1 large
Watermelon, 1 cup

NOTE: We recommend that you eat whole fruit in preference to drinking fruit juices whenever possible. In that way you gain the healthful benefits of the pectin, which aids digestion. When you do drink fruit juices make sure they are the natural juices with no sugar or artificial sweeteners added. Watch your local markets and buy local fruits in season whenever you can find them. Add variety to your diet by trying the different melons and fresh fruits like kiwis and pineapples that are now shipped fresh to local supermarkets during the year.

Food Group 4: Dairy

Each serving provides 100 calories. The serving size is noted next to each food listed below.

Blue cheese, 1 ounce
Buttermilk, 1 cup (low-fat)
Colombo Lite Plain Yogurt, 1 cup
Cottage cheese (1% fat), ½ cup

Evaporated skim milk, ½ cup
Farmer cheese, 2 ounces
Goat's milk, ½ cup
Kefir, ½ cup

Low-fat milk (2%), ¾ cup
Nonfat dry milk (quantity
　needed to make 1 cup)
Other hard cheeses,
　1 ounce
Other semisoft cheeses,
　1 ounce
Part-skim mozzarella,
　1 ounce

Part-skim ricotta, ¼ cup
Pot cheese, ¼ cup
Powdered skim milk,
　⅓ cup
Skim milk, 1 cup
Swiss cheese, 1 ounce
Yogurt (plain, low-fat, ac-
　tive culture), ⅔ cup

NOTE: The nutrition program limits your dairy servings because even small helpings of dairy are high
in calories and fat. You will find a number of varieties of low-fat cottage cheeses and yogurt on su-
permarket shelves, and these, along with low-fat
milk and hard cheeses eaten from time to time,
should be all the dairy foods you require.

Food Group 5: Protein

Each serving provides about 50 calories. A serving is usually a lean, cooked portion. The size of the portion is noted
on the food list below.

Beef, 1 ounce
Chicken (white meat, no
　skin), 1 ounce
Clams, 5 pieces or 3 ounces
Cornish hen, 1 ounce
Crab, 2 ounces
Dried peas, beans, ¼ cup
　cooked
Egg, 1
Flounder, 2 ounces

Haddock, 2 ounces
Halibut, 2 ounces
Ham, 1 ounce
Herring, 1 ounce
Lamb, 1 ounce
Liver, 1 ounce
Lobster, 2 ounces
Mackerel, 1 ounce
Mussels, 5 pieces or
　3 ounces

Navy beans, ¼ cup
Other legumes, ¼ cup
Oysters, 5 pieces or
 3 ounces
Peanut butter (natural),
 2 teaspoons
Pinto beans, ¼ cup
Pork, 1 ounce
Red beans, ¼ cup
Salmon, 1 ounce
Sardines, 1 ounce
Scallops, 5 medium pieces
Shrimp, 5 small pieces
Sole, 2 ounces

Soybeans, ¼ cup
Sunflower seeds, 1 table-
 spoon
Sprouts, 1 cup
Swordfish, 2 ounces
Tofu, 1 2-inch square
Tongue, 1 ounce
Trout, 2 ounces
Tuna (water-packed),
 2 ounces
Turkey (white meat, no
 skin), 1 ounce
Veal, 1 ounce
Venison, 1 ounce

NOTE: Limit beef servings to four ounces (when cooked, the portion will be about the size of a woman's fist). That will use up 4 portions of your daily protein allowance. Please be aware that it takes 2 ounces of fish (as opposed to 1 ounce of meat) to provide 50 calories. So eating fish enables you to have larger servings and still stay within your daily limit. You may want to increase your intake of this food item.

Food Group 6: Healthful Desserts, Snacks, Condiments, and Beverages

Each serving provides about 100 calories. The size of each serving is noted on the food list below.

Almonds, 15
Apple butter, 3 table-
 spoons
Avocado, ¼ medium

Brazil nuts, 4
Butter, 1 tablespoon
Carob or cocoa powder,
 4 tablespoons

Carrot juice (unsweetened),
8 ounces
Cashew nuts, 8
Decaffeinated teas, 2 to
3 cups
Filberts, 12
*Frozen yogurt, ½ cup
Frozen fruit bar, 1
Hazelnuts, 12
*Light beer, 12 ounces
*Liquor, 1 ounce
*Mayonnaise, 1 tablespoon
Miso soup, 3 cups
Molasses (blackstrap),
4 tablespoons
Oil (olive, safflower, soy,
etc.), 1 tablespoon
Oil-and-vinegar dressing,
2 tablespoons
Olives, green, 14; Greek,
4; ripe, 6
Pecans, 12 halves

Pine nuts, 12
Pistachio nuts (fresh, un-
salted), 35
Popcorn (air-popped),
1 quart
Pumpkin seeds, ⅔ ounce
*Regular beer, 8 ounces
Rice cakes (large size), 3
Rice Dream Frozen Des-
sert, ½ cup
Sesame seeds, ⅔ ounce
Squash seeds, ⅔ ounce
Sunflower seeds, ⅔ ounce
Tomato juice (unsweet-
ened), 16 ounces
Vegetable juice (unsweet-
ened), 16 ounces
Walnuts, 12 halves
Water-processed decaffein-
ated coffee, 2 to 3 cups
Wheat germ, ¼ cup
*Wine, 3 ounces

*Limit your intake to 2 servings per day (less is preferred).

Miscellaneous

The following foods may be consumed in unlimited
amounts and need not be counted into your plan.

Chives
Club soda
Coffee substitutes (grain
beverages)
Dulse
Garlic
Ginger root
Herbal teas (nonmedicinal)

Lemon
Lime
Mustard
Oat bran
Other herbs and spices
Red chili peppers
Rice bran
Seltzer water

Tamari soy sauce (light variety), used sparingly
Vinegar

Water, bottled or tap, at least 6 to 8 8-ounce glasses daily
Wheat bran

NOTE: The snacks listed will make it possible to munch a bit between meals or to eat smaller and more frequent meals. But please heed this word of caution. Once you start eating nuts, it's hard to stop, so limit yourself and be sure that you choose unsalted nuts, raw rather than roasted.

You'll find mayonnaise on this food list. One tablespoon of mayonnaise equals one portion and you need to count mayonnaise as a portion when you use it on sandwiches or salads. Note that herbs and spices also are included in this list and that they do not count as a food portion. Be sure to use herbs and spices to add variety and interest to recipes.

This is a sample day's menu for our 5'6" woman of small frame with a recommended weight of 125 pounds. As previously noted, her daily food list consists of the following:

Food Group 1: 6 servings
Food Group 2: 4 servings
Food Group 3: 2 servings
Food Group 4: 1 serving
Food Group 5: 5 servings
Food Group 6: 2 servings

Breakfast

V8 juice = 1 serving of Group 1 (Vegetable)
Hot or cold cereal, 1 cup = 1 serving of Group 2 (Carbohydrate)
Skim milk, ½ cup = ½ serving of Group 4 (Dairy)

Lunch

1 cup minestrone soup = 1 serving of Group 1 (Vegetable)
Tuna salad on whole-wheat toast with lettuce and tomato:
2 servings of Group 2 (Carbohydrate) and 1 serving of Group
5 (Protein)
½ serving of Group 1 (Vegetable)
Carrot and celery sticks = ½ serving of Group 1 (Vegetable)
1 apple = 1 serving of Group 3 (Fruit)

Dinner

1 baked potato topped with yogurt = 1 serving of Group
2 (Carbohydrate) and ½ serving of Group 4 (Dairy)
4 oz. of baked chicken = 4 servings of Group 4 (Protein)
1 cup steamed broccoli = 1 serving of Group 1 (Vegetable)
Mixed salad, 2 cups = 2 servings of Group 1 (Vegetable)
2 Tbsp. salad dressing of oil and vinegar = 1 serving of
Group 6 (Desserts, Snacks, Beverages)
1 3-ounce glass of wine or Tofutti = 1 serving of Group 6
(Desserts, Snacks, Beverages)

Bedtime snack

1 fruit or fruit juice = 1 serving of Group 3 (Fruit)

Understanding Vitamins and Minerals

The Bio-Nutrionics Nutrition Plan provides you with a
high-quality balanced vitamin and mineral intake. But the
only one who really knows how closely you are adhering
to the recommended foods and food lists is you. *If you do
not get the required amount of vitamins and minerals every
day in the foods you eat, you need supplements.* They are
important to overall health.

Everyone's Nutritional Needs Are Different

Although we advise supplementing your diet with vitamins and minerals we cannot, in good conscience, recommend specific dosages. Everyone's nutrient requirements differ; there simply is no such thing as a biochemically average person. You may consider yourself nutritionally "normal," but if you are a smoker, a contraceptive pill user, a person on medication or under emotional stress, or someone working in an unhealthy environment, your vitamin and mineral needs are probably very different from those of your neighbors.

The rational way to take vitamins is first to determine your requirements, then decide how much of those requirements is provided by the foods you eat. You make up the difference with supplements.

There's Nothing Better Than a Healthy Diet

As we mentioned before, while vitamins and minerals are extremely important to good health, they cannot take the place of a balanced diet. That is what the food plan is all about. It is the heart of Bio-Nutrionics and you will refer to this chapter again and again over the next thirty days. Eventually you'll learn the food lists and their values by heart.

4

Putting the Nutrition Plan to Work

Tip Sheet

Here is a variety of valuable tips. Some will save you time and money; others will help you understand the foods allowed on the Nutrition Plan and offer interesting ways to include them in your daily diet.

On Stock

Many recipes call for stock of one kind or another, either chicken, fish, meat, or vegetable. We recommend the homemade variety, which is easy and inexpensive to make (see directions below). To make a strong homemade stock, save the broth from chicken or fish that has been poached and store the broth in separate containers in the freezer. When you're ready to make chicken or fish stock, add the stored containers to the recipe. If you own a Crock-Pot you can begin your stock in the evening and let it cook overnight. Otherwise use any large pot. If you use canned stock, make sure it's low-sodium.

Chicken Stock: Place inexpensive pieces of chicken, such as the neck, back, and wings, or the carcass of a roasted chicken, or both, in a large pot or Crock-Pot. Cover the pieces of chicken with water and any reserved chicken broth you may have in your freezer. Add to this a couple of stalks of celery, including the tops; a cut-up, cleaned not peeled carrot; a bay leaf; and a peeled medium onion, cut in half. If you have small packets of mixed herbs, toss 'em in. Add about ten whole peppercorns. Bring to a boil and let simmer for at least an hour. Taste for flavor. Add salt substitute if necessary. Drain. Store and freeze for later use. Before serving, skim fat off top.

Fish Stock: Proceed as you would for chicken stock, replacing the chicken parts with fish heads and bones. (The exception to this rule is lobster heads. Do not use them in the preparation of a seafood stock.) To increase the strength of the stock, you can add a bottle of clam juice, but be careful of its sodium content. If you are on a low-sodium diet, omit clam juice.

Meat Stock: Ask your butcher for two to three pounds of beef and veal bones. You may have to pay for them, but the cost will be slight. Place bones in a moderate oven, at about 350°, and let the bones roast until nicely brown. Remove and discard the fat that accumulates in the pan. Put the bones in the Crock-Pot or large pot and proceed exactly as you would for chicken stock.

On Fish

The rule to follow for cooking fish is 10 minutes per inch of thickness. For example, if the fish is only a half-inch thick, it will require 5 to 6 minutes to cook, regardless of whether you are broiling, baking, or sautéing it.

Try new varieties of fish. There's an oceanful to draw

from, and you may be surprised how you'll come to love the different delicate flavors.

According to a study by the U.S. Department of Agriculture, the fat content of different types of fish varies considerably. Get to know the fatty fishes from the lean as it will help guide you in preparation. Lean fish has less than 2 percent fat. Cod is a good lean fish, as are others in the cod family: haddock, scrod, whiting, and pollack; all these along with mackerel, which is in the moderate-fat category (between 2 percent and 6 percent), are all rich in Omega-3 oils. You'll find the leaner fish excellent for sauces and salad. Other species of fish like bass, pike, sole, halibut, perch, snapper, and rockfish are also lean.

In the fatty group (over 6 percent fat) are salmon, swordfish, fresh tuna, bluefish, and, as you may have guessed, butterfish. The fattier fish contains enough natural oil of its own and therefore requires little or no oil when cooking. This group is not to be avoided because of its higher fat content. In fact, try to eat the following varieties more often, since they are an even greater source of Omega-3 oil: herring, mackerel, halibut, salmon, rainbow trout, and sardines.

And who among us can exist without canned tuna, salmon, and sardines. We've come to depend on them over the years. But we ask that you buy tuna packed in water. Sardines usually come packed in oil, sometimes olive oil, but either way they do tend to have a high sodium content. To be safe, drain the can before using them. Sardines are extremely healthy; we've heard them called a "tonic for the heart."

On Labels

We cannot stress enough the importance of reading labels on the foods you buy. Labels contain information vital to your health. Not only will you find the calories per portion listed on most items today, but you will also find the sodium content. Many packaged goods also list amounts of fats, carbohydrates, potassium, and protein. And given the urgency of "cholesterol overload," we predict they will soon carry the cholesterol contents as well. Ingredients are listed in descending order of proportion. For example, the product contains the most of the first ingredient listed and the least of the last, with the ingredients in between in their respective proportions. Whenever possible buy low-sodium products, especially when our recipes call for them.

On Salads

What do you think of when you hear the word *salad*? A bunch of green things on a plate, dripping with dressing? Now's the time to use your imagination, to get creative! We've listed below some items to mix into your assorted greens to make your salad a melody of color and texture:

Kidney beans	Cannellini beans
Chick-peas	Chinese pea pods
Mushrooms	Beets
Walnuts, broken up	Artichoke hearts
Sunflower seeds	Scallions
Carrots	Hard-boiled egg whites
Broccoli florets	Fresh peas
Whole-wheat croutons	Bits of flaked tuna

These are but a few suggestions. Make your own additions using the food lists as a guide.

How to Assert Yourself in a Restaurant

The time is not too distant when restaurants will serve whole-wheat breads, offer brown rice in place of white, and include whole grains in place of refined flour products in their daily fare. But until then you are going to have to learn to be discriminating in the choice of foods you order when dining out.

Assertiveness training is in order if you have any desire to eat healthfully at a restaurant. It's very easy to quickly survey the menu, see what is offered, and order with the request that the sauces be omitted. Broiled fish or chicken, steamed vegetables, salads with oil and vinegar or a vinaigrette dressing, and fresh fruits for dessert will serve you well.

Menu Planning

Here is a week of sample meals as a guide to your menu planning.

Please understand that these are only suggestions. You have a whole universe of foods to choose from in the food lists in Chapter 3. For example, if you dislike tuna fish, find a substitute among the many selections offered. If hot cereal doesn't appeal to you or you don't have the time to prepare it, try our low-fat, low-calorie, High-Energy Breakfast Drink instead. It's breakfast for winners that takes seconds to prepare.

But be alert to the importance of a hot breakfast, especially oatmeal, which actually lowers cholesterol. Try to have it several times a week.

Starred foods can be found in the recipe section of the book.

The best thirst quencher in the world is water. After that, hot herbal tea is the recommended drink.

Breakfast

Day 1   tomato or V8 juice
oatmeal with skim milk
Whole-Wheat Bread,* toast with honey

Day 2   ½ grapefruit
        whole-grain cereal with skim milk
        ½ whole-wheat English muffin with Fruit Jam*

Day 3   apple juice
        Cream of Rice (preferably brown)
        toasted Five-Grain Bread* with Fruit Jam*

Day 4   1 slice of whole-wheat toast
        High-Energy Breakfast Drink*

Day 5   juice or ½ grapefruit
        yogurt with banana
        Cranberry Muffin*

Day 6   melon sections
        Griddle Cakes* with Strawberry Sauce*

Day 7   juice
        Almond Crunch Granola* with skim milk
        Bran Muffin (Shirley's)*

Lunch

Day 1   Chicken Salad* on Five-Grain Bread*
        garnish with lettuce and tomato
        fresh fruit cocktail

Day 2   tuna salad on whole-wheat bread
        carrot sticks

Day 3   Quick Chili*
        green salad
        corn muffin

Day 4   Tuna and Cannellini Salad*
        whole-wheat toast
        apple

Day 5   pasta salad
        Cranberry Muffin*
        fruit salad

Day 6   chef's salad with linseed oil dressing*
        Five-Grain Bread*

Day 7   Bean and Spinach Soup*
        green salad (see salad tips)
        Gelatin*

Dinner

Day 1   Fish Fillets with Mustard Sauce*
        brown rice
        Carrots Raspberry*
        Apple Raisin Crisp*

Day 2   Pennsylvania Dutch Vegetable Soup*
        green salad (see salad tips)
        Crème de Cream*

Day 3   Risotto alla Milanese* with chicken added
        green salad (see salad tips)
        fruit

Day 4   Carrot Curry Soup*
        Tofu Burger* on whole-wheat English muffin
        garnish with lettuce, tomato, and onion
        Banana/Strawberry "Ice Cream"*

Day 5   Stir-Fry Beef and Vegetables*
        brown rice
        Sugar-free Gelatin*

Day 6   Pasta Gretchen*
        Zucchini and Tomato Italian Style*
        fresh fruit salad

Day 7   Chicken in Cream Sauce*
         broccoli with lemon
         Paul's Potatoes*
         Mary Theresa's Corn Shortcake*

Stocking Up

Before beginning your new life plan to lowering cholesterol, check your larder against this list. Then stock up on some of these suggested products.

Breakfast Cereals

Hot
   Oatmeal (best choice)
   Mother's Oat Bran
   Wheatena
   Cream of Wheat (preferably whole wheat)
   Cream of Rice (preferably brown rice)
Cold
   Granola, unsweetened
   Nutri-Grain
   Shredded Wheat
   Puffed wheat, corn, or rice

Breads and Crackers

   Whole-wheat pita bread
   Whole grain breads (available at health-food stores)
   Whole-wheat English muffins
   Finn Crisps
   Rice cakes
   Wasa Lite Rye
   Ideal Flatbread
   100% whole-wheat matzo

Beans, Rice, and Grains

Any fresh or dried beans, peas, and lentils (pinto, kidney, navy, and white (cannellini) are among those suggested)
Brown rice, long- and short-grain
Whole-wheat flour
Wheat germ
Unprocessed bran
Buckwheat groats (kasha)
Corn chips
Corn or flour tortillas
Pasta: wholewheat, spinach, artichoke, or pasta made with semolina, if others are not available

Fish, canned

Tuna, packed in water
Sardines, packed in water or olive oil
Mackerel
Salmon

Sauces and Salad Dressings

Prego No-salt Spaghetti Sauce
Ronzoni Lite Natural Marinara Sauce
Paul Newman's Marinara Sauce
Aunt Millie's Marinara Sauce
Dijon-style mustards
Vinegars, red and white wine, balsamic, cider, raspberry, etc.
Paul Newman's Italian Dressing
Hain's natural French, eggless Mayo
Old El Paso, Ortega, or Tio Sancho Taco, Salsa and Hot Sauces
Linseed oil (Hain's—obtainable at health-food stores)
Olive oil
Safflower oil

Walnut oil
Sesame oil
Tamari Lite Soy Sauce
Herbs, assorted dried (look for packets that can be im-
    mersed in soups)

Soups

Various bean, pea, and legume types with first choice
    given to those types with a vegetarian, nonmeat base.
    Also suggested is minestrone, vegetable, tomato,
    Manhattan clam chowder, mushroom barley, low-
    sodium chicken broth, or onion soup: Progresso,
    Health Valley, and Campbell's are brands to look for.
    Always check the label to see if the product is low
    in sodium.

Miscellaneous

Salt substitutes (Vegit, Season-Al, or Mrs. Dash)
Dried fruits
Walnuts
Raisins
Sunflower seeds, unsalted

In the "Fridge"

Yogurt, plain low-fat
Milk, skim
Farmer cheese
Cottage cheese, low-fat
Ricotta, low-fat
Mozzarella, part-skim
Fruit, assorted in season
Salad greens
Salad accompaniments (see tips on salads)

Recipe Index

Breakfast

Almond Crunch Granola
Griddle Cakes
High-Energy Breakfast Drink

Soups

Pennsylvania Dutch Vegetable Soup
Bean and Spinach Soup
Carrot Curry Soup

Main Dishes

Tofu Burger
Quick Chili
Fish Fillets with Mustard Sauce
Stir-Fry Beef and Vegetables
Spiced Chicken Salad
Chicken in Cream Sauce
Tuna and Cannellini Salad

Rice, Pasta, Grains, and Bread

Five-Grain Bread
Whole-Wheat Bread
Risotto alla Milanese (Italian Rice)
Pasta Gretchen
Shirley's Bran Muffins
Cranberry Bread

Vegetables

Zucchini and Tomato Italian Style
Carrots Raspberry
Paul's Potatoes

Sauces and Salad Dressings

Strawberry Sauce
Linseed Oil Dressing
Sweet-and-Sour Sauce

Desserts

Sugar-free Gelatin
Apple Raisin Crisp
Banana/Strawberry "Ice Cream"
Crème de Cream
Mary Theresa's Corn Shortbread
Flaky Pie Crust

Miscellaneous

Fruit Jam

Important Note

A breakdown of the number of portions of each of the six food groups is included for each recipe.

Breakfast

Almond Crunch Granola

2 Tbsp. sesame oil
¼ cup maple syrup or honey
6 cups rolled oats
¼ cup chopped almonds

Mix the oil and honey or maple syrup together. (Cinnamon and vanilla extract can be added in the oil-honey mixture for taste, if desired.) Stir in oats and almonds. Bake on a cookie sheet at 300° until golden and crisp. Let cool and store in a jar in a dark, cool place.
Serves 12.

Each serving is made up of:
1 Grain portion
1¼ Healthful Dessert portions

Griddle Cakes

½ cup whole-wheat flour
⅛ cup wheat germ
⅛ cup unprocessed bran
½ cup skim milk
1 egg white
⅛ tsp. tamari
oil to coat pan

Place all ingredients in food processor or blender and blend thoroughly. Coat griddle pan with oil. Drop batter by tablespoons onto pan, turning once. Serve with Strawberry Sauce.
Makes 10 griddle cakes.

Each 3-griddle-cake serving is made up of:
1 Grain portion

High-Energy Breakfast Drink

8 oz. skim milk
1 small banana, or 1 small apple, cored with skin left on
1 Tbsp. wheat germ
1 Tbsp. unprocessed bran
vanilla, dash

Place all the ingredients in a blender or food processor and blend well.
Serves 1.

Each serving is made up of:
with banana: 2½ Fruit portions, 1 Dairy portion
with apple: 2 Fruit portions, 1 Dairy portion

Soups

Pennsylvania Dutch Vegetable Soup

6 cups water
1 lb. lean beef, from flank or foreshank
2 sliced onions
2 stalks celery, cut in one-inch slices
4 pared beets, sliced to equal 2 cups
4 carrots, sliced thin
1 small cabbage, cut in wedges
1 bay leaf
1 cup beets, grated
2 tsp. salt substitute
1 6-oz. can tomato sauce, low-sodium
1 Tbsp. honey
2 Tbsp. white vinegar
½ pint low-fat yogurt

Place water, beef, onion, celery, *sliced* beets, carrots, cabbage, bay leaf, and salt substitute in large stockpot. Cover and simmer about 2 hours. Add grated beets, tomato paste, honey, and vinegar. Simmer 15 minutes more.

Up to this point the soup can be made the day before. Cool and refrigerate.

To serve, skim off fat and bring to a boil over medium heat. Lower heat and simmer, covered, for 10 minutes. Top with a dollop of yogurt before serving.

This soup freezes well.

Serves 8.

Each serving is made up of:
    1 Protein portion
    3 Vegetable portions

Bean and Spinach Soup

1 cup dried white beans
2 qts. boiling water
1 bay leaf
1 medium onion, chopped
1 clove garlic, chopped
2 Tbsp. olive oil
2 cups water
2 low-sodium beef bouillon cubes
1 16-oz. package frozen chopped spinach, or 1 lb. fresh
　spinach, if available
1 Tbsp. flour blended with 2 Tbsp. cold water
　freshly ground pepper

Cover beans with 2 quarts boiling water. Add bay leaf.
Cover pot and let stand for 1 hour. Sauté onion and garlic
in 2 tablespoons of oil until transparent. Add to bean pot
and simmer until the beans are soft, about 2 hours.

Add the water, bouillon, and spinach. Bring to boil and
stir in the flour-and-water mixture slowly. Grind in fresh pepper to taste. Taste for flavor. If necessary add salt substitute.
Serves 4.

Each serving is made up of:
　1 Grain portion
　1 Vegetable portion

Carrot Curry Soup

2 Tbsp. oil, preferably olive
2 medium onions, chopped
1½ Tbsp. curry powder
2 lbs. carrots, peeled and sliced
　dash of tamari or low-sodium soy sauce
¼ cup chopped fresh coriander or 1 Tbsp.
　dried

1½ quarts chicken stock, preferably homemade or low-sodium
2 cups plain yogurt (if soup is to be served
cold)
1½ cups skim milk (if soup is to be served
hot)
scallions or parsley for garnish

Heat oil in saucepan and cook onions until transparent.
Blend in curry powder and sauté for about 3 minutes. Add
carrots, tamari or soy sauce, coriander, and stock. Bring to
a boil and simmer for 20 minutes. Turn soup into food
processor or blender and purée. You may have to do this
2 cups at a time to avoid overloading.

If soup is to be served hot, return to pan, add milk, and
heat.

For cold soup, refrigerate after puréeing. Blend in yogurt
before serving. Garnish with thinly sliced scallions or
chopped parsley.

Serves 8.

Each serving is made up of:
1 Dairy portion
1 Vegetable portion

Main Dishes

Tofu Burger

30 oz. tofu
6 Tbsp. grated carrots
4 Tbsp. chopped scallions
2 Tbsp. sesame seeds
½ cup whole-wheat flour
2 Tbsp. tamari
3 Tbsp. peanut oil for sautéing

Mash tofu with a fork until crumbled. Combine tofu, grated carrots, chopped scallions, sesame seeds, flour, and tamari. Knead all ingredients well as if kneading bread. Shape dough into 8 patties. Heat oil in skillet. Sauté patties in hot oil until both sides are golden brown. Drain on absorbent paper. Serve on whole-wheat bread or whole-wheat rolls.

Tofu Burgers may also be broiled, after first brushing with oil.

Garnish with mustard, tomato, ketchup, lettuce, pickles, onion rings.

Serves 8.

Each serving is made up of:
  ¼ Healthful Dessert portion
  2 Protein portions

Quick Chili

    2 15-oz. cans of red kidney beans, drained
    1 1-lb. can of stewed tomatoes, low-sodium,
      if available
  1½ Tbsp. chili powder
    6 shakes of Tabasco sauce
    1 Tbsp. garlic, minced
    1 Tbsp. cumin
    2 shakes salt substitute
    2 oz. port or red wine
    1 medium onion, chopped

Place all ingredients in saucepan and stir together. Heat until all flavors are blended and hot.

Serves 2 as a main dish; 4 as a side dish.

Each serving is made up of:
  5 Grain portions
  1 Vegetable portion

Variations: To make this dish into Chili con Carne, add ¼ lb. of lean chopped meat sautéed in one tablespoon of olive oil.

For a cool creamy flavor, top with a dollop of yogurt.

Fish Fillets with Mustard Sauce

3 Tbsp. Dijon mustard
2 Tbsp. cider vinegar
1 tsp. honey
4 Tbsp. olive oil
1 Tbsp. chopped fresh dill
1 Tbsp. low-fat yogurt
1 lb. fish fillets. Use any firm-fleshed white fish, such as scrod, flounder, sole, monk, or cod.

In a small bowl combine mustard, vinegar, and honey. With wire whisk add oil a tablespoon at a time. Mixture should be thick. Fold in dill and yogurt. Let marinate for at least half an hour.

Wash fish off and pat dry with paper towels. Coat pan lightly with oil. Coat fish heavily with the marinade. Bake in preheated 350° oven until fish flakes easily, about 10 minutes. Place under broiler to brown top.

This dish may be broiled instead of baked. Place pan about 4 inches from broiling unit so as not to burn.

Tip: Save any leftover marinade to use as a salad dressing.

Add more yogurt to thin.

Serves 3.

Each serving is made up of:
    1 Healthful Dessert portion
    3½ Protein portions

Stir-Fry Beef and Vegetables

3/4 lb. lean boneless round beef
2 tsp. olive oil
2 tsp. sesame oil
1/3 cup carrots, sliced on the diagonal
1/3 cup onions, sliced
1/3 cup celery, sliced on the diagonal
5 to 6 mushrooms, cut in quarters
3 oz. Chinese pea pods, fresh or fro-
    zen (1/2 of 6-oz. package)
2 cups fresh bean sprouts
1/2 Tbsp. cornstarch
1/2 tsp. ground ginger
1 clove garlic, mashed
1 Tbsp. soy or tamari sauce
1/4 cup sherry

Trim fat from beef and slice into thin strips. Heat olive oil in wok and add beef over moderately high heat, turning until meat is no longer red. Remove and reserve. Add sesame oil to pan and heat. Add carrots and stir-fry 1 to 2 minutes. Add onion, celery, mushrooms, pea pods, and bean sprouts, and continue to stir-fry until vegetables are tender but still crisp, about 3 to 4 minutes.

Mix cornstarch, ginger, and garlic with soy sauce and sherry in small container until smooth and slowly add to vegetables, stirring constantly. Return beef to wok, reduce heat, cover pan for a minute for flavors to blend.

Serves 4.

Each serving is made up of:
  (beef)
    1 Healthful Dessert portion
    3 Protein portions
    1 Vegetable portion

(chicken)
    ½ Healthful Dessert portion
    3 Protein portions
    1 Vegetable portion

Spiced Chicken Salad

    1 cup cooked brown rice
    ¼ cup low-fat yogurt
    1 Tbsp. honey
    1 tsp. grated lemon peel
    ¼ tsp. ground ginger
    1½ cups cooked chicken*, cubed
    ¾ cup grapes, cut in half
    ¼ cup almonds, slivered, unsalted

Cook rice (⅓ cup of raw rice to ⅔ cup of water will make 1 cup of cooked rice). Combine yogurt, honey, lemon peel, and ginger. Stir into rice, fold in chicken, and top with grapes and almonds.
Serves 4.
*Use previously baked or poached chicken.

Each serving is made up of:
    ½ Grain portion
    1 Healthful Dessert portion
    3 Protein portions

Chicken in Cream Sauce

    2 Tbsp. olive oil
    ½ tsp. garlic, minced
    2 boneless chicken breasts, skinned and cut in half to
        make four pieces
    1 Tbsp. flour, whole-wheat if possible
    ½ cup skim milk
    ½ cup chicken broth, low-sodium

herb seasoning mixture
juice of half a lemon

Heat oil in skillet and add garlic and chicken. Cover pan and let cook for 15 or 20 minutes until tender and brown. (Cooking time depends on the size of the chicken breasts.) Remove to heated platter to keep warm.

While the chicken is cooking, place the flour and milk in a jar with a tight lid and shake well. Add it to the skillet after the chicken is removed and stir with a wire whisk. This will get quite thick. Quickly add the broth and continue to stir. Add seasoning and lemon juice. Stir again and return the chicken to the skillet, cover pan, and heat through for a couple of minutes so the flavors can blend.
Serves 4.

Each serving is made up of:
  1 Healthful Dessert portion
  3 Protein portions

Tuna and Cannellini Salad

  2 20-oz. cans of white cannellini beans
  2 7-oz. cans of albacore tuna, packed in water
  ½ cup chopped onions
  ¼ cup chopped parsley
  1 small carrot, chopped
  2 Tbsp. olive oil
  4 Tbsp. fresh lemon juice
    freshly ground pepper, to taste

Rinse beans thoroughly in cold water and drain. Pat dry. Drain tuna and flake. Chop onions, parsley, and carrot in food processor. Combine with tuna and beans. Add oil, lemon juice, and pepper and toss gently.
Serves 6.

Each serving is made up of:
2 Grain portions
¾ Healthful Dessert portion
1 Protein portion
¼ Vegetable portion

Rice, Pasta, Grains, and Bread

Five-Grain Bread

1½ cups boiling water
¾ cup cracked wheat (bulgur)
1 cup buttermilk
¼ cup molasses
2 Tbsp. honey
4 Tbsp. safflower oil
1 tsp. light tamari
2 envelopes dry yeast
¼ cup very warm water
2 cups white flour
½ cup bran
½ cup wheat flakes
2 cups whole-wheat flour
1 egg, beaten
1 Tbsp. poppy seeds

Pour boiling water over cracked wheat. Let stand for 1 hour. Heat together the buttermilk, molasses, honey, oil, and tamari. Stir and cool to lukewarm. Sprinkle yeast over ¼ cup warm water. Let proof for 10 minutes. Add to buttermilk mixture along with white flour and beat for 2 minutes until smooth. Stir in cracked wheat, bran, and wheat flakes. Slowly add whole-wheat flour, stirring until a nice firm dough is formed. Turn onto floured surface and knead 10 minutes until elastic and shiny. Add more white flour if necessary to keep from sticking. Place in large oiled bowl and let rise in warm place until doubled in volume. Punch down, knead on floured surface a few times, then let rest for 10 minutes. Divide and shape into two loaves. Place in greased pans, cover, and let rise again until doubled. Brush top with beaten egg and sprinkle with poppy seeds. Bake at 350° for 45 minutes until well browned.

Yields 2 loaves, 20 slices per loaf.

Each serving is made up of:
  1 Grain portion
  ½ Healthful Dessert portion

Whole-Wheat Bread

6 cups whole-wheat flour
1 package active dry yeast
1 tsp. salt (optional)
2 cups water
¼ cup safflower oil
2 Tbsp. honey

Mix 2 cups of the flour with yeast and salt. Heat water and oil together until warm (105°–115°). Add honey and stir into flour. Beat well. Mix in enough of the remaining flour to make a soft dough that leaves the side of the bowl. Knead on a lightly floured surface until dough is smooth and elastic, about 15 minutes. Place dough in a greased bowl and turn over once to grease upper side of dough. Cover and let rise in a warm place (80°–85°) until double in size, about 1 hour. Grease two 9 × 5 × 3 loaf pans. Press dough down to remove air bubbles. Divide dough in half, shape, and place in pans. Cover and let rise in a warm place until double in size, about 50 minutes. Place in preheated 375° oven. Bake until bread sounds hollow when tapped, about 30 minutes. Remove bread from pans and cool on rack.

Servings: 16 slices per loaf.

Each serving is made up of:
1½ Grain portions
½ Healthful Dessert portion

Risotto alla Milanese

This is an adaptation of a classic Italian dish. Prepared with brown rice it will have a crunchy consistency rather than a creamy one. Also, brown rice requires longer cooking and more liquid, so be prepared with a bit more stock. The dish is marvelous "as is," but you can make it a meal-in-one by adding a cup of cooked chicken, turkey, shrimp, or meat at the end and heating it through.

½ cup chopped onions
2 Tbsp. olive oil
1½ cups uncooked short-grain brown rice
¼ cup of Marsala wine (optional)
4–5 cups strong, hot chicken or vegetable stock, either homemade or low-sodium
⅛ tsp. powdered saffron
½ tsp. white pepper
½ cup part-skim mozzarella cheese, cut in small cubes
salt substitute (optional) and pepper, to taste
1 Tbsp. Parmesan cheese, grated

In a large skillet cook onions in olive oil 2 to 3 minutes until transparent. Stir in rice with a fork. Add wine at this point if using. Add 2 cups of hot stock to rice and continue stirring. Add saffron. Add more stock as liquid is absorbed. This process will take about 30 minutes. When all the liquid is absorbed and the rice tastes tender and crunchy, add mozzarella bit by bit. Season with salt, pepper, and Parmesan cheese.
Serves 6.

Each serving is made up of:
   3 Grain portions
   1 Healthful Dessert portion
   1 Dairy portion

Pasta Gretchen

2 lbs. fresh tomatoes, cut in cubes, seeded, not peeled
5 black olives, rinsed and sliced
2 oz. mozzarella cheese, cubed
1 3½-oz. can Italian tuna fish (see note)
2 tsp. oil from the tuna
2 Tbsp. olive oil
½ cup fresh basil, chopped
½ cup parsley, chopped
2 cloves garlic, chopped
   seasoning herbs (Vegit)
½ lb. angel hair or other thin pasta, preferably whole-wheat
2 Tbsp. Parmesan cheese, grated

Heat chopped garlic in 1 tablespoon of olive oil. Place tomatoes, olives, mozzarella cheese, tuna fish, tuna oil, remaining olive oil, basil, parsley, and garlic in a large bowl and allow to stand for at least one hour. Add seasoning herbs to taste.

Cook pasta according to package directions, making certain not to overcook. The pasta should be just barely done, or it will be mushy. Drain pasta and add reserved sauce. Top with Parmesan cheese.

Serves 4.

Note: If Italian tuna is not available, use regular water-packed tuna and add two teaspoons of oil to recipe. Italian tuna is packed in olive oil.

Each serving is made up of:
   1 Grain portion

2 Healthful Dessert portions
1 Protein portion
2 Dairy portions
1 Vegetable portion

Shirley's Bran Muffins

2 or 3 small or medium apples, cored, not
    peeled and cut in small pieces
3 eggs
¼ cup water
½ tsp. nutmeg
1 tsp. baking soda
1 tsp. baking powder
1 tsp. vanilla extract
1 tsp. cinnamon
¼ tsp. almond extract (optional)
2 cups unprocessed bran (either wheat
    or oat)

Combine apples, eggs, water, nutmeg, baking soda, baking powder, vanilla, cinnamon, and almond extract in a blender or food processor. After blending, pour contents into a bowl and stir in 2 cups of bran. Coat 12 muffin tins with safflower oil and spoon mixture into tins. Bake at 400° for 20 minutes.

Serves 12.

Note: Muffins should be refrigerated if not used at once. May also be frozen.

Each serving is made up of:
¼ Fruit portion
½ Grain portion

Cranberry Bread

2 cups whole-wheat pastry flour
2 cups unbleached white flour

1 Tbsp. baking powder
1 tsp. baking soda
1 tsp. salt (optional)
½ tsp. cinnamon
¼ tsp. nutmeg
½ cup sesame oil
1 Tbsp. grated orange rind
1½ cup orange juice, fresh
1 cup maple syrup
2 cups cranberries, fresh or frozen, unsweetened
1 cup chopped walnuts
⅔ cup raisins

Preheat oven to 350°.

Sift together the flours, baking powder, baking soda, salt (if using), cinnamon, and nutmeg. Add oil and stir in thoroughly. In a separate bowl combine orange rind, orange juice, and maple syrup. Add to flour-oil mixture. Fold in berries, nuts, and raisins. Divide batter and turn into two greased and floured 9×5 loaf pans. Bake at 350° 55 to 60 minutes. Cool and refrigerate. Slices better the next day.

Yields 2 loaves, 16 slices per loaf.

Each serving is made up of:
1 Fruit portion
1 Grain portion

Vegetables

Zucchini and Tomato Italian Style

1½ Tbsp. olive oil
1 medium onion, thinly sliced
1 clove garlic, minced
1 medium zucchini, thinly sliced
1 medium tomato, seeded and cut in chunks

½ tsp. dried basil
salt substitute
freshly ground pepper

Heat oil in large skillet. Add onions and garlic and cook for 2 minutes. Add sliced zucchini and sauté until zucchini begins to turn brown around edges. Add tomatoes and basil, stir and cook for 2 to 3 minutes. Add seasonings to taste.

Cover pan. Turn off heat and let stand for a few minutes to allow flavors to blend.

Serves 3.

Each serving is made up of:
½ Healthful Dessert portion
1¼ Vegetable portions

Carrots Raspberry

2 large or 3 medium carrots
2 Tbsp. water
1 Tbsp. unsalted butter
1 Tbsp. lemon juice
1 tsp. raspberry vinegar
½ Tbsp. honey

Peel and thinly slice carrots. In small covered saucepan, place carrots with 2 tablespoons of water and butter. Bring to a high heat and quickly lower heat. Cook 10 minutes or until just done. Watch carefully that the carrots don't burn. Add lemon juice, raspberry vinegar, and honey. Stir. Turn off heat. Shake pan with cover on and allow flavors to blend for 2 minutes and serve.

Serves 2.

Paul's Potatoes

¼ Tbsp. olive oil per person
1 medium potato per person

Coat surface of nonstick baking pan with olive oil. (Pan size depends on number of potatoes.) Wash potatoes and slice* about ¼ inch thick. Lay in single layer in pan. Bake at 350° until well browned.

*Potatoes may be cut French-style, shoestring, or, if you can cut them thin enough, into potato chips.

1 potato per serving.

Each serving is made up of:
1 Grain portion

Sauces and Salad Dressings

Strawberry Sauce

1 pint of strawberries*
2 Tbsp. honey
2 Tbsp. fruit liqueur (optional)

Clean berries and cut in half. (There should be about 2 cups.) Place berries in blender or food processor with honey and blend. Add liqueur and blend again. Serve on griddle cakes, gelatin, gingerbread.

Serves 8.

*Note: You may replace strawberries with raspberries. Out of season, use frozen berries to equal 2 cups.

Each serving is made up of:
1 Fruit portion

Linseed Oil Dressing

*Developed by Mrs. Joan Rudin and Dr. Donald Rudin, this dressing is highly recommended. Please be certain to use **only** linseed (flaxseed) oil obtainable only at health-food stores, and **not** the kind from hardware stores. Always refrigerate linseed oil.*

1 cup linseed oil (flaxseed)
⅓ cup vinegar
1 Tbsp. Dijon-style mustard
1 tsp. tamari
1 Tbsp. crushed, dried basil

Combine all ingredients and beat with a wire whisk or place in a jar with a tight cover and shake. *Always* refrigerate unprocessed oils.

Serves 20; each serving equals two tablespoons.

Each serving is made up of:
1 Healthful Dessert portion

Sweet-and-Sour Sauce

1½ cups unsweetened pineapple juice
½ cup plus 2 Tbsp. maple syrup
½ cup apple cider vinegar
¼ tsp. garlic powder
2 Tbsp. arrowroot

Combine juice, syrup, cider vinegar, garlic powder, and arrowroot in a saucepan over medium heat. Whisk out all lumps and beat, stirring constantly until thickened. Use over fish or chicken.

Makes 8 ¼-cup servings.

Each serving is made up of:
2 Fruit portions

Desserts

Sugar-free Gelatin

1 qt. fruit juice (any kind except citrus or pineapple)
½ tsp. cinnamon
2 packets plain gelatin
2 cups fresh fruit, chopped

Bring juice and cinnamon to a boil. Add gelatin and cook 5 minutes. Lay chopped fruit in the bottom of a 9 × 11 flat baking dish and pour gelatin mixture over it. Let cool and refrigerate until firm.
Serves 12.

Each serving is made up of:
1 Fruit portion

Apple Raisin Crisp

Topping
2 cups rolled oats
¼ tsp. salt
⅓ cup oil
½ cup honey

Mix oats, salt, and nuts together. Add oil and mix well. Add honey and mix to coat all ingredients.

Crisp
6 apples, cored and sliced
1 cup raisins
1 cup apple juice
¼ tsp. salt (optional)
1½ Tbsp. arrowroot (cornstarch) diluted in ¼ cup water
½ tsp. cinnamon
½ tsp. vanilla

Arrange sliced apples in a baking dish and set aside. Cook raisins in 1 cup apple juice with salt, if using, until soft. Thicken with diluted arrowroot. Sprinkle cinnamon and vanilla on apples, then pour on raisin sauce. Cover with topping. Bake at 350° for 40 minutes.
Serves 12.

Each serving is made up of:
    1 Fruit portion
    1 Grain portion
    1 Healthful Dessert portion

Banana/Strawberry "Ice Cream"

    4 large bananas, very ripe
    2 cups strawberries, cleaned and hulled

Freeze the bananas whole. Pare off skins with a knife and discard. Chop into small pieces and place in blender or food processor. Add strawberries. Begin at slow speed and add drops of water, enough to allow process. When completely whipped empty into freezer container and freeze until ready to serve.
Note: You may substitute raspberries or pineapple for the strawberries.
Serves 6.

Each serving is made up of:
    2 Fruit portions

Crême de Cream

    1 cup cold skim milk
    ½ cup powdered skim milk
    1 Tbsp. vegetable, almond, or walnut oil

Pour the fresh milk into blender at high speed. Add powdered milk a tablespoon at a time. Slowly add vegetable oil. Use at once or freeze. Use on gingerbread or other dessert.

Serves 6, 2 tablespoons per serving.

Each serving is made up of:
  ¾ Dairy portion

Mary Theresa's Corn Shortcake

    1½ cups cornmeal
    1½ cups whole-wheat pastry flour
    1 tsp. baking powder
    ½ tsp. cinnamon
    ⅓ cup sesame oil
    ¼ tsp. tamari
    ½ cup water
    ½ cup apple juice
    ¼ cup maple syrup or honey

Preheat oven to 350°.

Mix cornmeal, flour, baking powder, and cinnamon together in a bowl. With fingers rub the sesame oil into this mixture until all the oil is absorbed. In second bowl combine the tamari, water, apple juice, and maple syrup or honey. Add this mixture to the flour mixture and turn the whole into an oiled 7 × 7 baking pan. Bake for 40 minutes.

Serve with Strawberry Sauce (see page 73).

Serves 9.

Each serving is made up of:
  1½ Grain portions
  1 Healthful Dessert portion

Flaky Pie Crust (for 2 pies)

1 cup oat flour
2 cups whole-wheat pastry flour
1 Tbsp. arrowroot
½ cup butter
⅓ tsp. salt

Place flours and salt in a bowl. Grate butter into mixture and blend. Add water to form into a ball. Roll dough out to ¼″ thick. Bake at 375° for 8 to 10 minutes.
Serves 8.

Each serving is made up of:
2 Healthful Dessert portions

Miscellaneous

Fruit Jam

½ lb. dried fruit. Choose from dried apricots, dried peaches, dried apples, pitted prunes or raisins, or combine two or more to make ½ pound
2 cups water*
ginger or cinnamon, powdered, to taste

In a saucepan cook the fruit with 1½ cups of water until plump and juicy. Purée in a blender to make a smooth paste. Add seasoning to taste. Add remaining water and blend. Store in refrigerator.
Yields 2½ cups. Serving size: 2 tablespoons.
*You may replace part of the water with fruit juice.

Each serving is made up of:
1 Healthful Dessert portion

5

The Bottom Line

You Can Prevent Cholesterol Overload

Now it's your turn. Think of this as the first day of the rest of your life. Begin the preventive program that Bio-Nutrionics offers now and gain the benefits no matter what your age. Remember, no one knows when their cholesterol buildup begins or how rapidly it will progress. You can't feel it or see it. Doesn't it make better sense to alter your life-style now rather than trying to halt or reverse half a lifetime of artery damage after CHD has reached an advanced state?

It's Your Turn to Prove the Promise

Remember that for every 1 percent reduction in cholesterol, you decrease your risk for CHD by 2 percent. After just a few months on the program a 25 percent cholesterol reduction is a reality for many people. That means you will have cut your risk of coronary heart disease in half. We also guarantee you'll reach your maximum health potential—no matter who you are or what you do.

We hope you'll put our program to work right now—not for just a month but for a lifetime. Just give us a try and discover the difference between you . . . and you at your best.